Essential

INTUITIVE EATING

Guide to Recovery

An Innovative Anti-Diet Method with Rules for Nourishing a Healthy and balanced diet Relationship with Food for Daily Inspirations.

Elyse Evelyn Jackson

ISBN:

Printed in the United States of America

Disclaimer

This publication is designed to provide competent and reliable information regarding the subject covered. However, the views expressed in this publication are those of the author alone, and should not be taken as expert instruction or professional advice. The reader is responsible for his or her actions. The author hereby disclaims any responsibility or liability whatsoever that is incurred from the use or application of the contents of this publication by the purchaser of the reader. The purchaser or reader is hereby responsible for his or her actions.

Table of Contents

Introduction

Do you want to learn more about intuitive eating but are unfamiliar with it? Our SIMPLIFIED INTUITIVE EATING GUIDE TO RECOVERY walks you through the foundations, ten principles, research, benefits, common misconceptions and misunderstandings, and how to get started on the road to healing your relationship with food.

What Is Intuitive Eating, Exactly?

Intuitive Eating (IE) was created in 1995 by two dietitians, Elyse Resche and Evelyn Tribole, as an evidence-based health strategy. If you just remember one thing from this book, it should be that intuitive eating is not a diet. It's frequently referred to as an anti-diet. There are no prohibited foods. There are no limits on when what, or how much you can eat. A non-diet (or anti-diet) strategy focuses on health-promoting behaviors rather than assessing success based on a number on a scale. Others will assert Intuitive eating is a philosophy of eating that educates you to be an expert on your body's hunger signals. It is, in essence, the inverse of a traditional diet. It gives no suggestions on what to avoid or when to eat. Instead, it teaches you that you are the greatest — and the only — person to make those choices. IE, at its core, means returning to the way we were born to eat. We ate when we were hungry and stopped when we were full, which we understood instinctively by listening to our bodies cues. We were not born watching our meals, calculating our macronutrients, or counting calories, and we were not exposed to external forces telling us what we should and should not do to be healthy (or thin, as diet culture would have it). The impulse to eat or refrain from eating was entirely instinctual. Finding a way back to those internal cues is a critical component of intuitive eating. As a non-diet approach, IE means addressing both physical and psychological requirements, as mental health is just as crucial as physical health, and only you know what you need at any given moment. You have power over your own body. According to Resche and Tribole, intuitive eating is impact energy that can be utilized to break out from the dieting circle and weight obsession, as well as comprehend what it means and feels like to be in touch with nature and reconnect with food. It's okay if this feels overwhelming, tough, or even impossible! Eating intuitively is a skill that must be cultivated. It takes time to break down all of the diet limitations and sensations you may want to cling to. Consider how long you've been dieting or struggling with your food connection! You didn't create these behaviors overnight, and the healing process of IE won't either. That's why Resche and Tribole created the 10 Principles of Intuitive Eating, which are designed to help you with anything from detecting and rejecting diet culture to dealing with emotional eating to embracing gentle nutrition. We'll go over those concepts in greater depth later in this book. This book provides a thorough introduction to intuitive eating.

The Essentials

Intuitive eating is a method of eating that promotes a positive attitude toward food and one's body image. The idea is to eat when you are hungry and stop when you are full. Although this should be a natural process, it isn't for many people. Putting your trust in diet books and so-called experts on what, when, and how to eat may take you away from trusting your body and its instincts. You may need to relearn how to trust your body to eat intuitively. To do so, you must distinguish between physical and emotional hunger: There is physical hunger. This biological drive alerts you to the fact that you must refill your nutrients. It comes on gradually and involves a variety of symptoms, such as a rumbling stomach, tiredness, or irritability. It is fulfilled when you take any food. Thirst for emotional fulfillment. This is driven by an emotional desire. Sadness, loneliness, and boredom are just a few of the feelings that can lead to cravings for food, especially comfort foods. Eating causes feelings of guilt and self-hatred.

Intuitive Eating's Evolution

In 1995, Evelyn Tribole and Elyse Resch used the word "intuitive eating" as the title of a book. The concept, on the other hand, finds its origins in preceding notions. Early pioneers included Susie Orbach, who authored "Fat is a Feminist Issue" in 1978, and Geneen Roth, who has written about emotional eating since 1982. Green Mountain at Fox Run, a weight-control program in Vermont, was founded by Thelma Wayler in 1973. Diets, according to the program, are useless, and lifestyle changes and personal care are more important for long-term health. You've undoubtedly tried a few different diets and dieted before (or tried a diet disguised as a "lifestyle program"). As previously said, you probably lose weight. But the diet was so challenging to follow that you gave up, regained your weight, and possibly formed some disordered eating behaviors along the way. After a little interval, you decide that a different diet would be preferable, and the operation is restarted.

Yo-yo dieting entails going on and off diets regularly, which commonly leads to weight cycling (losing and regaining weight over and again), which may be hazardous to both physical and emotional health. Dieting also commonly requires extreme restrictions, often on both the quantity and kind of food ingested. When we don't get enough calories, our brain creates a hormone called Neuropeptide Y (NPY), which drives us to want carbs. As a result, our survival mechanism kicks in after a period of restriction, resulting in a binge. Clinically, a binge is defined as "consuming a quantity of food in a discrete-time that is greater than what most people would consume in a comparable length of time under similar conditions." There is frequently a sensation of loss of control. Afterward, you may feel extreme remorse and humiliation and vow to "do better" (aka limit better) the next day. This is the binge-restrict cycle that many dieters – and non-dieters – are subjected to. Many people think they have reached "diet rock bottom" and are no longer able to take it. In this instance, intuitive eating is useful. Intuitive eating is a method of breaking the cycle of yo-yo dieting, weight cycling, and binge-restricting. In truth, the primary principle of intuitive eating is to reject diet culture — to reject the idea that the next diet will be a success, and to reject the idea that weight is the be-all and end-all of health. IE is the antidote to the unhealthy and stressful practices that dieting entails. IE, on the other hand, teaches you how to eat the way you were meant to eat: by listening to your body, letting go of external rules, and establishing permanent harmony with food.

Who Can Participate in Intuitive Eating?

Anyone who has a body can try intuitive eating. Seriously. There are no qualifying conditions or prerequisites to fulfill to be eligible for the IE. You don't have to struggle with diets, weight loss, or any other unhealthy eating habits. Working with an eating disorder dietician who is also schooled in intuitive eating, on the other hand, maybe incredibly useful if you have a known eating issue. Food allergies, dietary limitations, and medical difficulties are all possible within the IE framework.

What Are the Benefits of Intuitive Eating?

Over 100 study articles have been published on the benefits of intuitive eating, with more being undertaken all the time. Positive health benefits that have a strong correlation include: Lower your total and LDL cholesterol levels. Reduce your triglyceride level. HDL levels have increased. Self-esteem that is high increased self-esteem Increased happiness as a result of greater life satisfaction Eating disorders and poor eating are less common.

What Makes Intuitive Eating So Appealing?

Let us begin with a summary of diet culture. Even if you are not on a diet, you are still a member of the diet culture world. It's easy to become caught up in this belief system, believing that thin = healthy, that reducing weight gives you a higher social standing, that some eating choices are horrible and others are OK, and that it's okay to stigmatize people who don't match one picture of health. Yes, that's a lengthy statement, but it's still tough to spot all of the subtle ways diet culture infiltrates our lives. More data about the hazards of dieting, particularly targeted weight loss, has lately reached the mainstream. Weight cycling (losing and regaining weight) has been associated with an increased risk of death compared to maintaining a steady weight. People with an "overweight" BMI (the BMI is a topic for another day) had the lowest risk of death and chronic disease among all BMIs. Finally, data suggest that weight stigma may cause more harm than simply being in a larger body. So, why do we keep dieting? Why do we continue to desire slim bodies while stigmatizing others? Eating culture.

Aside from the collateral harm, the larger point is this: diets don't work. "But," you may say, "I've lost weight on a diet." You'd be correct. However, it is also possible that you were unable to keep your weight reduction going. So, how successful was the diet? No! Diets, according to research, are not long-term. According to studies, two-thirds of dieters gain back more weight than they lost while on the diet. Furthermore, any short-term health benefits are transient. In actuality, as previously said, diets may be harmful to one's health.

The Ten Principles of Intuitive Eating

Rescue and Tribole, as previously noted, devised ten guiding principles of intuitive eating. Each has its chapter in the book and is just as important as the ones that come before and after it.

The idea is for you to go through each principle, taking the time to understand its relevance in the journey and working hard to put it into practice. There are no requirements that you follow these principles in any specific order - IE is not a linear process. However, gentle nutrition is the final principle on purpose since it will be difficult not to translate gentle nutrition principles into another diet or set of limitations if you haven't yet rejected diet culture or made peace with food.

1. Overcome the Diet Mentality

Dieting, the desire must lose weight, and the belief that being thin is superior are all instilled in us from a young age. How many different diets have you experimented with? Have they had any success? How long will this last? Did you feel better on the inside and out as a result of it? How long did you feel like that? They most likely "worked" for a time before stopping. The problem is with diets, not with you. You did not fail your diet or fail to become a better person because you did not lose enough weight. Diets, no matter how they are marketed to you, are ineffective. Work on rejecting the idea that dieting is the answer. Unfollow social media accounts that promote diets, weight loss, or diet culture. Remove any diet-related cookbooks. Surround yourself with weight-inclusive, body-positive messaging.

2. Be mindful of your hunger.

In diet culture, being hungry is celebrated. The hungrier you are, the "better" and more "willpower" you have. This is an unnatural situation for anyone to be in - hunger is a biological activity, and we require food to survive. To return to an earlier point, hunger plays a significant part in the binge-restrict cycle. The longer you restrict yourself, the more hungry you will become. Our bodies abhor being hungry, and eventually, our natural urge to survive takes over, resulting in severe cravings, an increased chance of bingeing, and a sense of being out of control with food. To become more intuitive with eating, first, recognize your hunger and all of its intricacies. Recognize your body's hunger cues and feed it what it requires.

3. Make Food Friendships

"I love ice cream, but I can't have it at home because I'll eat it all," some of my customers tell me. Ice cream is viewed as a "bad" food that should be taken in moderation in these cases. The fact is that the more you convince yourself you won't be able to eat something, the more you want it. According to studies, when we are introduced to a previously banned food, the pleasure areas of our brain light up more. Cravings will increase until they reach a peak, at which time you will consume the entire pint, if not more. Allow yourself to devour without hesitation. When you can eat ice cream anytime you want, the deprivation mentality fades, as do the intense cravings and bingeing.

4. Go toe-to-toe with the Food Police

Diets love to categorize things as good or bad, causing us to believe that we – as people – are either good or bad depending on what we consume. The fourth intuitive eating principle encourages you to reject such foolish rules. Say no to the food cops who tell you that the food you're eating is "bad" and that you should feel guilty or humiliated for eating it.

5. Calculate the Satisfaction Factor

Food is much more than just a source of energy. To feel completely pleased, you must also feel full. This is only feasible if you permit yourself to consume anything you want. Consider the last time you went to an Italian restaurant and ordered pasta but received fish instead. You'd had your fill, but were you satisfied? Unlikely, since it was not what your body or mind desired. Get the methods I use to calculate your enjoyment factor right here.

6. Be aware of your fullness

You must value your fullness just as much as you value your hunger. When eating any meal or snack, pay attention to how you're feeling. Do you want to eat anything else? Do you have an empty stomach? You may be aware of the discomfort that comes with being overly full, but there are many more nuances to fullness than the jammed sense. Learning to recognize hunger and fullness cues is a process; tuning into your body on this level will take some time.

7. Handle Your Emotions Kindly

To begin, it is critical to recognize that emotional eating is a normal and healthy coping mechanism. When emotions are high, it's also critical to develop tools other than eating, so that food becomes one of several coping talents from which to choose. You may also experience a variety of unpleasant sensations associated with eating, but you can begin to work with them by viewing them with love and self-compassion. If this notion is unfamiliar to you, read my post on how to practice self-compassion, in which I explain what self-compassion is, why it matters, and how you might practice it.

8. Be Mindful of Your Body

Every human body is unique, and they would remain so even if we all ate and exercised in the same way. Resche and Tribole use the following analogy: if you were a size 8, it would be difficult (and unpleasant!) to squeeze into a size 5 shoe. The same may be said for your physique. Instead of criticism and scorn, all bodies are entitled to equal respect and dignity. You don't have to adore your body, but you should respect it. Respecting your body entails being present for it, caring for it, and treating it with compassion.

9. Notice the Difference in Joyful Movement

I've written a lot about this since exercise is often co-opted by diet culture and is typically overlooked when it comes to disordered eating or eating disorders. Movement is beneficial to our physical and mental wellbeing, but too much of it can be fatal. Shift your focus from calorie burn to how it feels to work out. Choose an exercise that makes you feel happy, energized, hopeful, or even quiet (like light stretching). Don't do anything that makes you feel bad! Do you want to know more about the difference between pleasant movement and overexercise? I previously discussed why I stopped taking the stairs, and more recently, I went into length about fitspiration and the problems it brings.

10. Take Care of Your Health (Gentle Nutrition)

One of the most prevalent misconceptions about intuitive eating is that you will eat whatever you want, whenever you want. This idea is debunked by principle eleven, which states that nutrition is a crucial component of both IE and overall health. Making decisions that promote health and respect what makes you feel the best, both emotionally and physically, is what gentle nutrition is all about. It is beneficial to include fruits and vegetables in your diet regularly, but omitting a meal, a day, or even a week will not make or break your health. With this IE philosophy, we're taking a flexible approach to nutrition, stressing balance and diversity. Nutrition isn't about following tight rules or collecting data, which is why I don't provide nutrition facts on my recipes!

Where do I even begin?

If you feel you might benefit from learning more about intuitive eating, there are measures you can take.

Begin by analyzing your eating habits and attitudes objectively. Consider whether you are experiencing physical or emotional hunger when you eat.

If you have physiological hunger, assess your level of hunger/fullness on a scale of 1–10, from severely hungry to completely satisfied. Eat just when you're hungry, not when you're hungry. When you're pleased but not full, call it a day.

You may also learn more by following some of the professionals in the field:

The Intuitive Eating Book: This best-seller, written by Evelyn Tribole and Elyse Resch, promoted intuitive eating. It debuted in 1995 and has remained popular to this day.

The website of Evelyn Tribole, the Original Intuitive Eating Pro, contains further information about intuitive eating.

Geneen Roth (writer): Her website has useful information and videos, as well as a link to an online class.

Ellyn Satter Institute Ellyn Satter promotes an approach called "eating competency," which incorporates many aspects of intuitive eating.

To summarize

When it comes to intuitive eating, how you eat is just as important as what you eat. Allowing your internal hunger and fullness cues to guide your eating habits may improve your body image and overall quality of life.

www.ingramcontent.com/pod-product-compliance
Lightning Source LLC
La Vergne TN
LVHW052111160826
845678LV00015B/3480

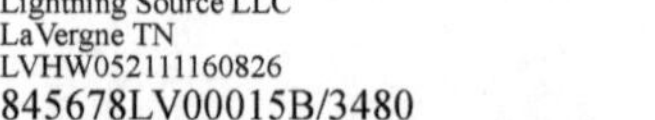

* 9 7 9 8 4 1 8 2 1 0 8 1 4 *